# Bulletpoints
# THE OLD TESTAMENT

First published in 2004 by Miles Kelly Publishing Ltd
Bardfield Centre, Great Bardfield
Essex, CM7 4SL

Copyright Miles Kelly Publishing Ltd

2 4 6 8 10 9 7 5 3 1

**Editorial Director:** Belinda Gallagher
**Picture Research:** Liberty Newton
**Production:** Estela Boulton

Produced by Cyber Media (India) Ltd
**Consulting Editors:** Rajiv Seth, Prashant Parida
**Editor:** Taru Agarwal
**Project Leader:** Sudhendu Kumar Singh
**Author:** Preethi Paul
**Designer:** Sheetal Ghambir

All rights reserved. No part of this publication may be reproduced, stored in a retrieval system, or transmitted by any means, electronic, mechanical, photocopying, recording or otherwise, without the prior permission of the copyright holder.

British Library Cataloguing-in-Publication Data
A catalogue record for this book is available from the British Library

ISBN 1-84236-495-2

Printed in China

www.mileskelly.net
info@mileskelly.net

The publishers would like to thank Anness Publishing for the use of their artwork
All other images: MKP Archives; Dover; PhotoDisc

# Contents

The Bible 4

Adam and Eve 6

Noah 8

Tower of Babylon 10

Abraham 12

Jacob 14

Joseph 16

Moses 18

The ten plagues 20

The Red Sea parts 22

Manna from Heaven 24

The Ten Commandments 26

Naomi and Ruth 28

Samson 30

David and Goliath 32

King Solomon 34

Daniel 36

Jonah 38

Index 40

# The Bible

- **The Bible** is a collection of 66 books that was written by more than 40 different authors, ranging from kings and philosophers to fishermen and peasants.
- **The term 'Bible'** means 'books,' and it is an entire library, with stories, songs, poems, letters, history, as well as literature, spread over a period of 1500 years.
- **The Bible was originally written** in three different languages: Hebrew, Aramaic and Greek. The New Testament and some of the books in the Old Testament were written in Greek.
- **The entire Bible contains** 1189 chapters that are divided into more than 3100 verses. The shortest verse in the Bible is 'Jesus wept.'
- **Today's Bible is divided into two parts**, the Old Testament and the New Testament, and has been translated into 2233 languages.

▲ *The Bible is the first ever mechanically printed book in the world.*

# The Old Testament

- **The Old Testament consists** of 39 books and is traditionally arranged into three sections: the Law, the Prophets and the Writings.
- **The Old Testament** is considered to be the Holy Scriptures for three major religions in the world, Islam, Judaism and Christianity.
- **In 1454, Johannes Gutenberg** invented the 'type mold' print press and printed the Gutenberg Bible, which was the first ever mechanically printed full-length book.
- **The *Guinness Book of World Records*** rates the Bible as the best-selling nonfiction book of all times.
- **It would take** about 70 hours to read the complete Bible.

▲ *Torah is the religious book for the Jews.*

# Adam and Eve

- **Genesis, the first book in the Bible**, details God's creation of the universe and of Man.
- **God created** Heaven and Earth, day and night, the Sun, Moon and the stars, the seas and the skies, plants and trees and birds and animals.
- **Adam and Eve**, the first humans created by God, lived in the Garden of Eden. Some archaeologists believe that the heavenly garden was situated near the Persian Gulf in the Middle East.
- **A stream flowed through the Garden of Eden**, and was divided into four rivers called Tigris, Euphrates, Pishon and Gihon.
- **There were two trees** in the middle of the Garden of Eden, the Tree of Life and the Tree of Knowledge of good and evil. God had forbidden Adam and Eve to eat fruits of the Tree of Knowledge.
- **Satan**, in the form of a serpent, tempted Eve and Adam to eat the forbidden fruit.
- **When Adam ate the fruit**, it got stuck in his throat. That is why the apple-like voice box (larynx) in the throat is also called the Adam's Apple.
- **After they ate the forbidden fruit**, Adam and Eve became aware of their nakedness and covered themselves with fig leaves.
- **God sent Adam and Eve away** from the Garden of Eden because they had disobeyed Him.
- **The epic poem, Paradise Lost**, by John Milton, describes the temptation by Satan and the expulsion of Adam and Eve from the Garden of Eden.

# The Old Testament

▶ *An angel with a flaming sword guarded the Tree of Life and prevented Adam and Eve from returning to the Garden of Eden.*

# Noah

- **God was unhappy** with the sinful ways of His people and decided to destroy all life forms on earth, by causing rain for 40 days and nights.
- **Noah**, who was 600 years old, was a righteous person and God instructed him to build an ark (a big boat), take his family and at least two of each kind of animal into the ark.
- **Some people, called Arkeologists**, claim to have found most of the remains of Noah's ark on Mt Ararat in Turkey.
- **After the ark was built**, God gave His people seven more days to repent, but to no avail.
- **It began raining heavily** and the whole world was covered with water, drowning everyone, except for Noah, his family and all the animals inside the ark.
- **An English archaeologist, Sir Leonard Woolley**, proved that there was a massive flood near the Persian Gulf around 4000BC, but no one knows if this is the same flood that the Bible mentions.
- **The rain stopped and 150 days later**, Noah sent out a dove, and when it returned with a fresh olive leaf, he knew the land was dry.

### ...FASCINATING FACT...
There was a girl named Noah, as well!
A man named Zelophehad had five daughters,
one of whom was called Noah. (Joshua 17:3)

## The Old Testament

- **Noah, his wife, his three sons Shem, Ham and Japheth,** and their wives came out of the ark, built an altar and offered burnt sacrifice to God.
- **God made a covenant** (promise) with Noah that He would never destroy the world with a flood again, and sealed this covenant with a rainbow.
- **All the descendants of Adam** perished in the great flood except for Noah and his family.

▲ *The ark was said to be 137 m long, 22.8 m wide and 13.7 m high, with three decks. The dimensions of the ark are similar to the huge ocean liners we find today.*

# Tower of Babylon

- **Noah's descendants** settled in a plain in Babylon, in the East. They were very prosperous and proud.
- **Babylon was a flourishing city**, and the hanging gardens of Babylon are one of the seven wonders of the ancient world.
- **As a city**, Babylon was both envied and loathed.
- **The story of the tower of Babylon** explains the presence of different languages in the world, in spite of the fact that all the people were descendants of Noah.
- **The people wanted to prove their power** over God by building a tall tower that reached up to the sky.

> **FASCINATING FACT**
> Another tower, the Eiffel Tower of Paris, is one of the seven wonders of the modern world.

- **In history, there are many accounts** of an unfinished tower in Babylon.
- **The tower of Babylon** was technologically sophisticated for the ancient times; it was made of baked bricks and mortar.
- **God made the people speak different languages** all at once, and they could not understand each other.
- **The people were confused**, and as a result, they could not complete the tower.

▶ *Babylonians could not complete building the tower because God confused them by making them speak different languages.*

The Old Testament

# Abraham

- **Abraham and his wife, Sarah**, did not have any children, yet God promised and blessed him to be the father of many nations.
- **God promised the land of Canaan** for Abraham's numerous descendants.
- **Abraham** had a son named Isaac when he was 100 years old and Sarah 90.
- **Father Abraham** is the founder of Judaism and is also revered by both Christians and Muslims.
- **God commanded Abraham** to take young Isaac to a mountain and offer him as a sacrifice, and Abraham obeyed.
- **God was touched by Abraham's faith** and prevented him from killing his beloved son.
- **Abraham sacrificed a ram** instead of Isaac.
- **Muslims commemorate this act of faith** by sacrificing goats during the festival of Bakrid.
- **The name 'Isaac'** means 'he laughs,' and 'Sarah' means 'princess' in Hebrew.

▲ *Abraham built an altar and was about to sacrifice Isaac when an angel of God appeared and stopped him.*

## The Old Testament

▼ *The angels warned Abraham before destroying the sinful city of Sodom.*

**··· FASCINATING FACT ···**
Abraham was earlier known as 'Abram' until God blessed him to be the father of many nations.

# Jacob

- **Jacob and Esau** were twin sons of Isaac and Rebecca.
- **Jacob** had very smooth skin and Esau was hairy all over.
- **Jacob tricked** his blind old father into blessing him by covering his body with goatskin, much to the anger of Esau.
- **Jacob dreamt** of a stairway that reached up to heaven, with hosts of angels on either side, and God blessed him in the dream with numerous descendants.
- **Jacob met Rachel**, fell in love with her and worked for many years for Rachel's father to win her hand in marriage.
- **Many years later**, Jacob met his brother, Esau, and they made peace with each other.
- **On the way to meet Esau**, Jacob wrestled with a man all night and was badly hit on the hip.

## The Old Testament

- **This man was actually God** and He blessed Jacob and renamed him as 'Israel'.
- **Jacob had two wives**, Rachel and Leah who were sisters.
- **Jacob had 12 sons** and each tribe of ancient Israel was named after them.

◀ When Jacob and Esau met many years later, Esau had 400 men with him, while Jacob had a big family of 12 sons, two wives and many maids.

# Joseph

- **Joseph was Jacob's favourite son** among his 12 children.
- **Jacob gifted Joseph** a beautiful long coat with many colours, much to the jealousy of other sons.
- **Joseph had dreams** that revealed that his brothers and parents would bow down in front of him and Joseph would rule over them.
- **Joseph's brothers dropped him into a dry well** and dabbed goat's blood on his coat to convince Jacob that wild animals had killed his son.

▲ *Joseph's brothers realized their mistake and begged for forgiveness.*

- **Reuben, the eldest brother**, decided not to kill Joseph; instead they took him out and sold him to some traders.
- **Joseph became a slave** of the Pharaoh's officer, Potiphar, but he was imprisoned after Potiphar's wife falsely accused him.
- **Joseph was very good in interpreting dreams** and was freed from prison to help the Pharaoh understand dreams.
- **Joseph explained two of the Pharaoh's dreams** and warned him that Egypt would be struck by a famine.

The Old Testament

- **The Pharaoh was pleased** with Joseph and appointed him as the governor of Egypt.
- **The Pharaoh** also made Joseph in charge of food supplies when the famine affected Egypt.
- **Joseph's brothers and Jacob** came to Egypt to live with him.

▼ *Joseph's brothers were so jealous of him that they plotted to kill him by dropping Joseph into a dry well.*

# Moses

- **The Israelites living in Egypt** were forced to become slaves and were treated badly by the Egyptians.

- **The cruel Pharaoh ordered** that all newborn Hebrew children should be put to death.

- **Moses was born to a Hebrew woman** who hid him for three months, and then made a reed basket, placed baby Moses in it and floated him in the river Nile.

- **The Pharaoh's daughter** saw the baby in the reed basket, picked him up and adopted him as her own son.

- **When Moses grew up**, he saw Egyptians treating Hebrews cruelly, even killing them.

- **Moses had to flee** from the royal palace because he killed an Egyptian who was ill-treating Hebrews.

> **FASCINATING FACT**
> Moses received the Ten Commandments from God, on Mt Sinai.

- **God appeared to Moses** in the form of a flaming bush and commanded him to lead the people of Israel out of Egypt.

- **God gave Moses** a magical walking stick that could turn into a snake and had many other miraculous powers.

- **God appointed Aaron**, Moses' brother, to help Moses to save the Israelites.

- **Moses and Aaron** went to Egypt with their families, to free Israelites from slavery.

The Old Testament

▶ Moses's mother and sister waited by the river Nile until the Pharaoh's daughter found him.

# The ten plagues

- **Moses and Aaron** asked the cruel Pharaoh to release the Israelites so that they could go to the desert and worship God, but the Pharaoh refused.
- **The land of Egypt** was struck by ten plagues that created havoc to the people living there.
- **Moses and Aaron** turned the water of the river Nile into blood and the people had no water to drink; even then the Pharaoh did not give up.
- **Moses and Aaron used their powers** to infest the land of Egypt and the river Nile with frogs, but the Pharaoh refused to let the Israelites go.
- **God continued to send more plagues** in the form of gnats and flies that covered living spaces in Egypt.
- **All the livestock** that belonged to the Egyptians died of terrible diseases and the people had sores and boils.
- **When God saw that the Pharaoh was still unrelenting**, He sent the worst hailstorm that had ever struck Egypt.
- **A huge swarm of locusts** destroyed all the crops in the country.
- **God covered the sky** over Egypt with thick clouds of darkness, but the land where the Israelites lived still had light.
- **In the final plague**, God passed over the land of Egypt and all the first-born children of both humans and animals perished, but the Israelites were unharmed.
- **The Pharaoh** finally let the people of Israel go away from Egypt.

▶ *Swarms of locusts covered Egypt and destroyed every grain of food.*

# The Old Testament

# The Red Sea parts

- **God wanted the Pharaoh** to let His people go to the desert to worship Him, but the Pharaoh refused.
- **God wanted to punish the Egyptians** by killing all the first-born offsprings of humans and animals.
- **Each Israelite household** sacrificed a lamb and smeared its blood on the doorpost.
- **The mark helped God** recognize the homes of His people and spare the Israeli first-borns when He passed over Egypt.
- **This event is commemorated** as the Jewish Passover feast and the Jews eat unleavened bread on this day.

> **FASCINATING FACT**
> The Red Sea is red because it has algae, which turn reddish-brown when they die.

- **The Pharaoh released the Israelites** after ten plagues affected the land of Egypt.
- **The Pharaoh and his army** pursued the Israelites when they realized that they were not coming back to Egypt after praying in the desert.
- **Moses raised his hand** and the waters of the Red Sea parted into two walls.
- **The Israelites crossed the sea** safely, and the sea closed in and swallowed the Egyptians who followed them.

The Old Testament

▼ *The Red Sea miraculously opened up for the Israelites to pass through.*

# Manna from Heaven

- **Moses led the Israelites** from Egypt to find their promised land, Canaan.
- **The Israelites camped** in the desert, and two months later, began to complain for food.

◀ *God caused it to rain Manna from heaven to feed His people while they wandered in the desert.*

- **God decided to feed** His people for the rest of the time they were in the desert.
- **The Israelites** wandered in the desert for 40 years.
- **A large flock of quails** flew into the Israeli camp and provided meat for the people.
- **There was dew** all over the camp and when it evaporated, thin flaky bread appeared.

## The Old Testament

- **This bread was called Manna** and tasted like cakes made of honey.
- **The people were supposed to collect Manna** that would be sufficient for one meal and not more than that.
- **Some people tried to collect more than they could eat** and store it, but the Manna rotted and turned into worms.
- **When the people were thirsty** and could not find water in the desert, Moses struck a rock with his walking stick and water gushed out of it.

◀ *In the evenings, quails flew in and provided meat for the Israelites.*

# The Ten Commandments

- **God appeared to Moses** on Mount Sinai in the form of clouds and smoke.
- **Moses** was given the Ten Commandments on two stone slabs.

▶ *God wrote The Ten Commandments on two stone slabs.*

## The Old Testament

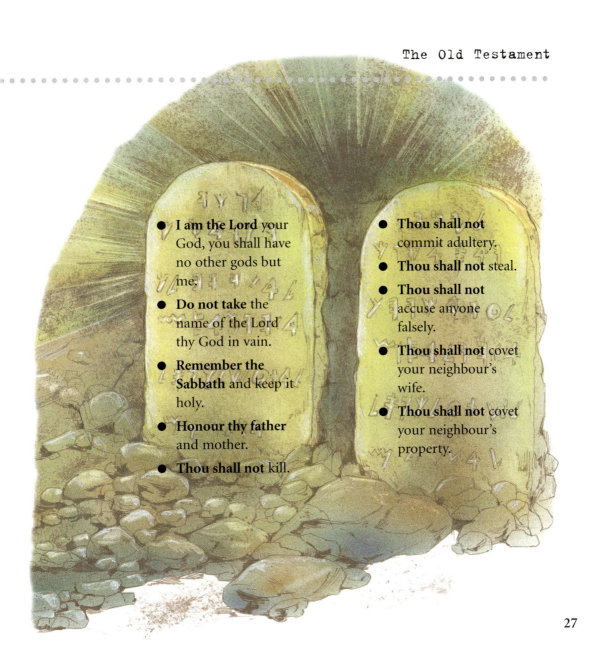

- **I am the Lord** your God, you shall have no other gods but me.
- **Do not take** the name of the Lord thy God in vain.
- **Remember the Sabbath** and keep it holy.
- **Honour thy father** and mother.
- **Thou shall not** kill.
- **Thou shall not** commit adultery.
- **Thou shall not** steal.
- **Thou shall not** accuse anyone falsely.
- **Thou shall not** covet your neighbour's wife.
- **Thou shall not** covet your neighbour's property.

# Naomi and Ruth

- **Naomi was a widow** from Bethlehem who lived in the country of Moab.
- **Naomi had two sons** named Mahon and Chilion, who married Moabite women, Orpah and Ruth.
- **Orpah and Ruth** also became widows, and Naomi decided to go back to Bethlehem.
- **Naomi asked her daughters-in-law to stay back in Moab**, go to their parents' homes, remarry and lead their own lives.
- **Ruth did not leave Naomi** and decided to go to Bethlehem with her, while Orpah left them tearfully.
- **Ruth followed Naomi** all the way home and worked in the fields of a rich and influential man named Boaz.
- **Boaz, who was Naomi's relative**, was a kind man and had heard about Ruth's kindness.
- **Boaz married Ruth** despite the fact that she was a foreigner because she stayed with her old mother-in-law and took care of her.
- **Ruth and Boaz were blessed** with a son named Obed.
- **Ruth became the great-grandmother** of David, Israel's greatest king.

> **FASCINATING FACT**
> The television celebrity Oprah actually got her name by misspelling 'Orpah'.

The Old Testament

▶ Orpah left Ruth and Naomi and went back to her parents' home.

29

# Samson

- **Samson**, who was born to Manoah and his wife, was a Nazirite and did not cut his hair or drink wine.
- **Samson fell in love** with a Philistine girl and wanted to marry her.
- **A very strong person**, Samson killed a lion on his way to meet her, and on his way back, found honey inside the lion's body.
- **At his wedding reception**, Samson challenged the guests to solve a riddle about the lion. He said, "Out of the eater came something to eat, out of the strong came something sweet. What is it?"
- **Samson became furious** when his wife revealed the answer to the guests, and he caught 300 foxes, tied two each by their tails, set them on fire and sent them into the Philistine fields.
- **The Philistines tied him** with sturdy ropes and tried to stop him but he broke all the ropes.
- **During the tussle**, he found the jawbone of a dead donkey lying nearby; he picked it up and killed a thousand Philistine men with it.
- **Later, Samson fell in love with another Philistine girl, Delilah**, who persuaded him to reveal the secret of his strength — his long, uncut hair.
- **Delilah told the Philistines** about Samson's secret and they cut his hair, tied him to pillars and blinded him.
- **Samson prayed to God** for strength, pushed the pillars and the building fell down, killing many Philistines.

▶ *Delilah found out the secret of Samson's strength and told the Philistine kings about it.*

# The Old Testament

# David and Goliath

- **David was a young shepherd** who was good at playing the harp.
- **David was appointed** in the palace to play the harp for the old king, Saul.
- **The Philistines** wanted to conquer Israel and challenged the Israelites to defeat Goliath, a member of the Philistine army.
- **Goliath**, who was nine feet tall, wore heavy bronze armour and carried a powerful spear on his shoulder, challenged the Israelites for 40 days.
- **King Saul** declared that anyone who killed Goliath would be rewarded handsomely and could marry his daughter.
- **David was in the king's camp** at that time because he wanted to meet his brothers who were in the army.
- **David asked the king's permission** to fight Goliath, went to the nearby stream, collected some pebbles and readied his sling.
- **Goliath laughed scornfully** when he saw young David challenging him with a sling and some pebbles.

▲ *David used five smooth pebbles and his sling to kill Goliath the giant.*

## The Old Testament

- **David hit Goliath** with a pebble, and when the giant fell down dead, David ran to take his sword and chopped off his head.
- **David wrote** many of the psalms present in the Bible.

▼ *David hit Goliath on the forehead and broke his skull with a sling and stone.*

# King Solomon

- **King Solomon**, the son of King David, was one of the most prosperous and wise kings of Israel.
- **King Solomon's wealth and wisdom** was so well known that famous people like the Queen of Sheba came to see him.
- **Two women**, who were fighting over a baby, wanted the king to judge who the real mother was.
- **King Solomon ordered** that the baby should be cut into two halves and given to the women.
- **The real mother pleaded** that she would rather give up the baby than kill it and the king found out who was the real mother.
- **King Solomon built** many splendid palaces and a grand temple.
- **He dedicated** the temple to God and called it the Temple of the Lord.
- **The Israelites built the Temple of the Lord** 480 years after Moses led them out of Egypt.

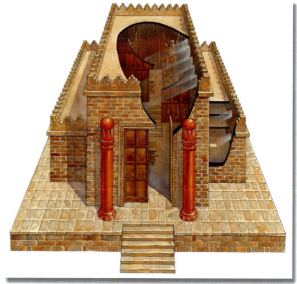

▲ *The Temple of the Lord had many rooms and was decorated with cypress and cedar wood and gold.*

## The Old Testament

- **King Solomon wrote** and collected 3000 proverbs and wise sayings, and was also the author of 1005 songs.
- **King Solomon had about a 1000 wives**, including the Pharaoh's daughter.

▼ *The just and wise King Solomon helped the mother get her baby back.*

# Daniel

- **The king of Babylonia** captured the city of Jerusalem where Daniel lived.
- **Daniel helped** the king interpret his dreams and predict the future, and this helped the king to be a just ruler.
- **Daniel was a very powerful person** in the kingdom because he was close to the king and many of the king's officials were jealous of him.
- **The jealous officials plotted to kill Daniel**, but they could do nothing against him because he was very honest and just.
- **The officials** praised the king and requested him to ask the people of his kingdom to only worship him for the next three days.
- **The king ordered** that anyone who did not follow his instructions would be thrown into a pit of hungry lions.
- **Daniel refused to worship** anybody else other than God and he continued his prayers like before.
- **The officials told** the king about Daniel's disobedience.
- **Daniel was thrown into the pit** of hungry lions for a whole night, but he came out unharmed.
- **The king understood** that Daniel was falsely accused, punished the jealous officials and put them to death.

▶ *The king threw Daniel into a pit with hungry lions and closed it with a huge stone.*

# The Old Testament

# Jonah

- **God asked Jonah** to go from Galilee to Nineveh, the capital of Assyria, with His message.
- **Assyria and Israel** were bitter enemies, and Jonah did not want to go to Nineveh.

▼ *The sailors cast lots to find out who had disobeyed God and threw Jonah out of the ship.*

- **Jonah disobeyed God** and boarded a ship to go to Tarshish (earlier Spain) and as far away from God as possible.
- **A very violent storm broke out** on the way, and the sailors in the ship were convinced that someone aboard the ship had disobeyed God.

## The Old Testament

- **Jonah confessed** that he was trying to run away from God, and if they threw him overboard, the storm would calm down.
- **The sailors threw Jonah** out of the ship and a whale swallowed him.
- **Jonah remained inside the whale** for three days and three nights, praying and repenting.
- **After three days**, the whale spat Jonah out on a beach, and he decided to go to Nineveh.
- **Jonah warned the people of Nineveh** that God would destroy their city if they did not repent for their sins.
- **The people realised their mistakes** and changed their sinful ways.

▶ A whale swallowed Jonah, and yet, he miraculously escaped death.

# Index

Aaron 18, 20
Abraham 12
Adam and Eve
    Garden of Eden 6
    forbidden fruit 6
Adam's Apple 6
altar 8
archaeologist 6, 8
ark 8
Arkeologists 8
Assyria 38

Babylonia 36
Bakrid 12
Bethlehem 28
Bible
    Aramaic 4
    Gutenberg Bible 5
    Holy Scriptures 5
    library 4
    New Testament 4
    Old Testament 5
blood 16, 20, 22
Boaz 28
bread 24

Canaan 12, 24
Christians 12
covenant 8
creation 6

Daniel 36
David 34
Delilah 30
descendants 8, 10, 12, 14
desert 20, 22, 24
diseases 20
dove 8
dream 16, 36

Egypt 18, 20, 22, 24, 34
Egyptian 18, 22
Esau 14
Euphrates 6

famine 16
fishermen 4

flaming bush 18
flood 8
foxes 30

Galilee 38
Genesis 6
Gihon 6
goatskin 14
governor 16
Greek 4
*Guinness Book of World Records* 5
Gutenberg, Johnnes

hair 14, 30
hanging gardens 10
harp 32
Hebrew 4, 12, 18
honey 24, 30
hosts of angels 14

Isaac 12, 14
Islam 5
Israel 15, 18, 32, 35, 38
Israelite 18, 20, 22, 24, 32, 34

Jacob 14, 16
Japheth 8
Jerusalem 36
John Milton 6
Judaism 5, 12

king 4, 36
kingdom 36

languages 4, 10
larynx 6
lion 30, 36

Manoah 30
Middle East 6
Moab 28
Moabite 28
mortar 10
Moses 20, 24, 26, 34
Mount Sinai 26
Mt Ararat 8

Muslims 12

Nazirite 30
Nineveh 38
Noah 8, 10

Orpah 28

Paradise Lost 6
Passover feast 22
people 8, 10, 18, 20, 22, 24
Persian Gulf 6, 8
Pharaoh 16, 18, 20, 22, 35
Philistine 30
Philistines 32
philosopher 4
Pishon 6
Potiphar 16
proverbs 35
psalms 33

quails 24
Queen of Sheba 34

Rachel 14
rainbow 8
Rebecca 14
reed basket 18
religion 5
Reuben 16
riddle 30
river Nile 18, 20
ruler 36

sacrifice 8, 12, 22
Sarah 12
Satan 6
Saul 32
serpent 6
seven wonders 10
Shem 8
ship 38
slavery 18
sling 32
song 4, 35
steal 27
storm 38

sword 33

Tarshish 38
Temple of the Lord 34
temptation 6
ten plagues
    boils 20
    first-born 20, 22
    flies 20
    frogs 20
    gnats 20
    hailstorm 20
    livestock 20
    locusts 20
    sores 20
Tigris 6
tower of Babylon 10
Tree of Knowledge 6
Tree of Life 6
Turkey 8
twin 14
type mold 5

uncut hair 30
universe 6
unleavened bread 22

verses 4

walking stick 18, 25
whale 39
widow 28
wine 30
Woolley, Sir Leonard,
worship 20, 36
wrestle 14